Symphony No. 35
in D Major, K385, "Haffner"

❄

Symphony No. 36
in C Major, K425, "Linz"

❄

Symphony No. 38
in D Major, K504, "Prague"

Wolfgang Amadeus
MOZART

DOVER PUBLICATIONS, INC.
Mineola, New York

LIZ KALANJA (216-754-2591)
HELENA KOPCHICK

Published in Canada by General Publishing Company, Ltd., 30 Lesmill Road, Don Mills, Toronto, Ontario.

Published in the United Kingdom by Constable and Company, Ltd., 3 The Lanchesters, 162–164 Fulham Palace Road, London W6 9ER.

Bibliographical Note

This Dover edition, first published in 1998, is a republication of Symphonies Nos. 35, 36, and 38 in "Serie 8. Symphonien," Vol. 3, of *Wolfgang Amadeus Mozart's Werke, Kritisch durchgesehene Gesammtausgabe,* originally published by Breitkopf & Härtel, Leipzig, in 1880–1882.

International Standard Book Number: 0-486-40420-X

Manufactured in the United States of America
Dover Publications, Inc., 31 East 2nd Street, Mineola, N.Y. 11501

CONTENTS

INSTRUMENTATION

Symphony No. 35
"Haffner"

2 Flutes [Flauti]
2 Oboes [Oboi]
2 Clarinets in A [Clarinetti]
2 Bassoons

2 Horns in D, G [Corni]
2 Trumpets in D [Trombe]

Timpani

Violins I, II [Violino]
Violas [Viola]
Cellos and Basses
   [Violoncello e Basso]

Symphony No. 36
"Linz"

—
2 Oboes
—
2 Bassoons

2 Horns in C, F
2 Trumpets in C

Timpani

Violins
Violas
Cellos and Basses

Symphony No. 38
"Prague"

2 Flutes
2 Oboes
—
2 Bassoons

2 Horns in D, G
2 Trumpets in D

Timpani

Violins
Violas
Cellos and Basses

Symphony No. 35

in D Major, K385, "Haffner" (1782)

I

44

50

73

80

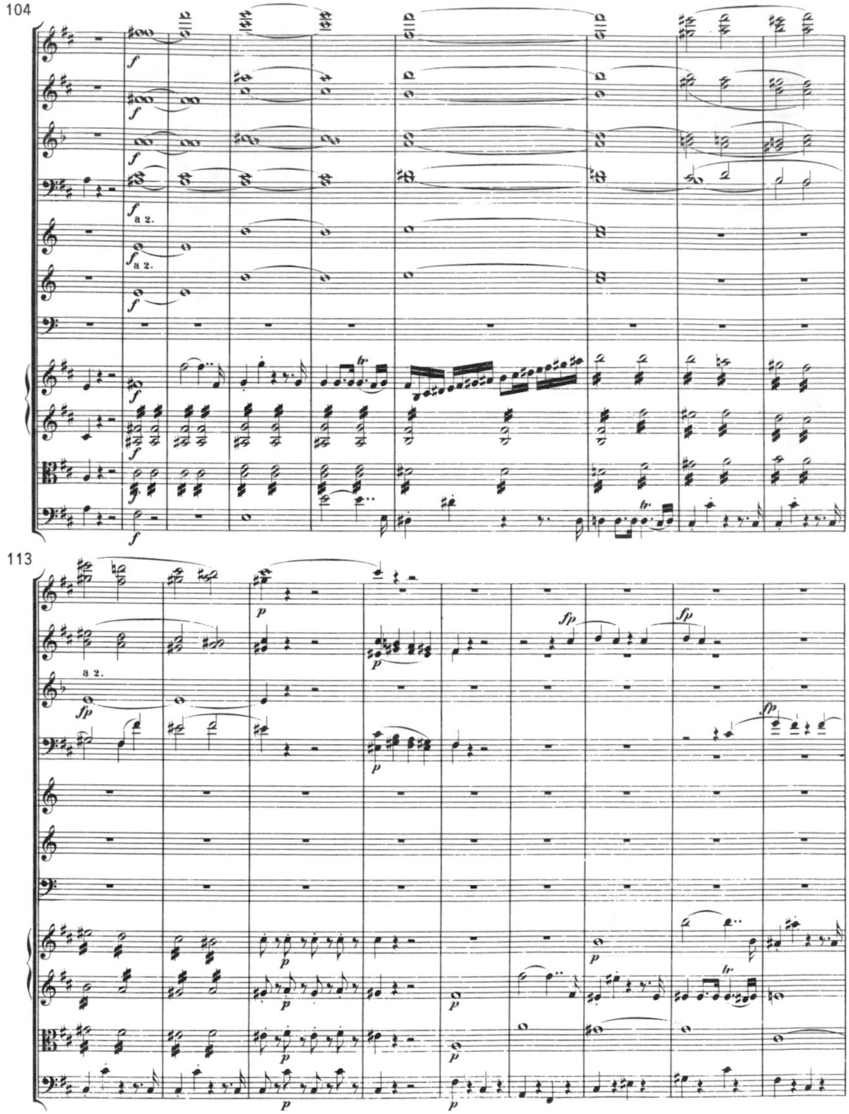
104
a 2.
a 2.
113
a 2.

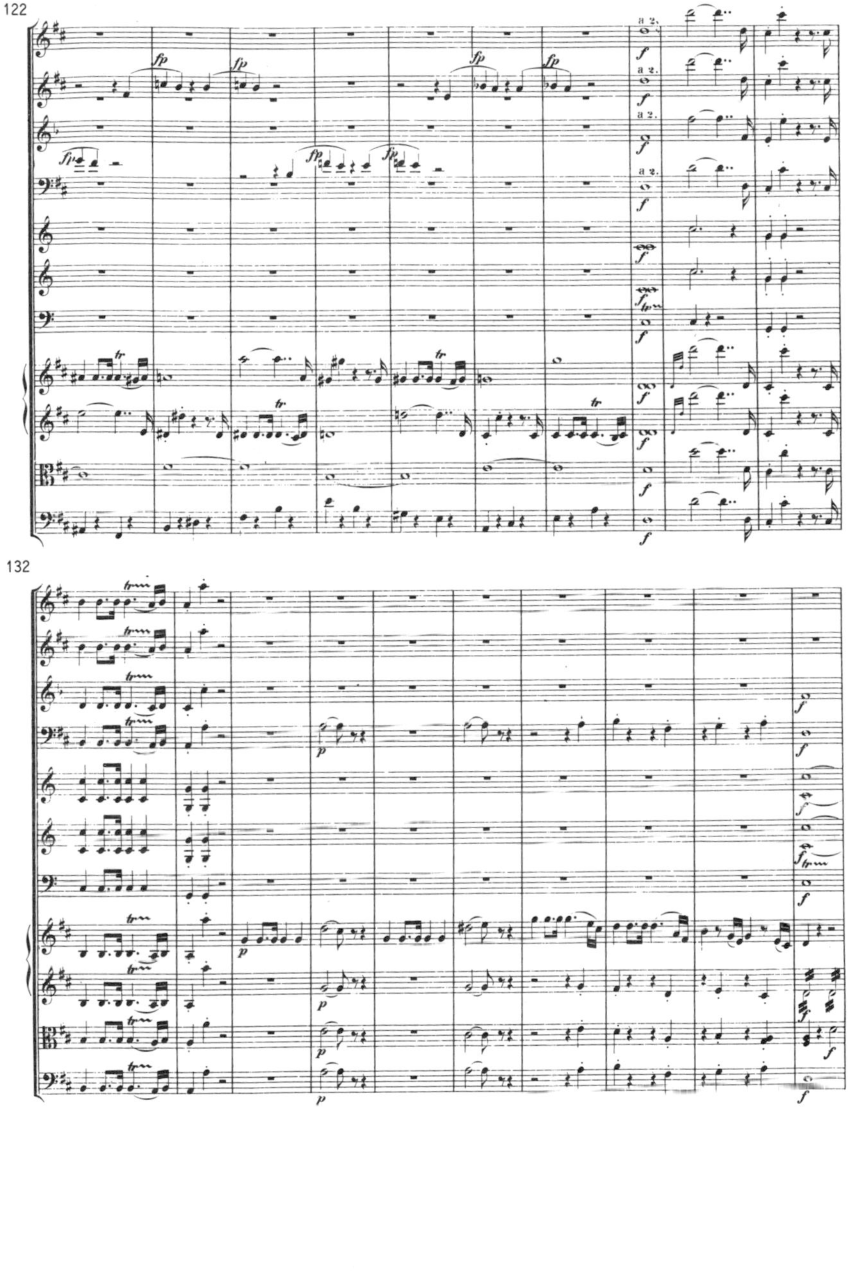
122
a 2.
fp
f
tr
132
p

155

163

II

	Andante.
Oboi.	
Fagotti.	
Corni in G.	
Violino I.	
Violino II.	
Viola.	
Violoncello e Basso.	Andante.

14

III

11

25

Trio.

Menuetto da Capo.

IV

22

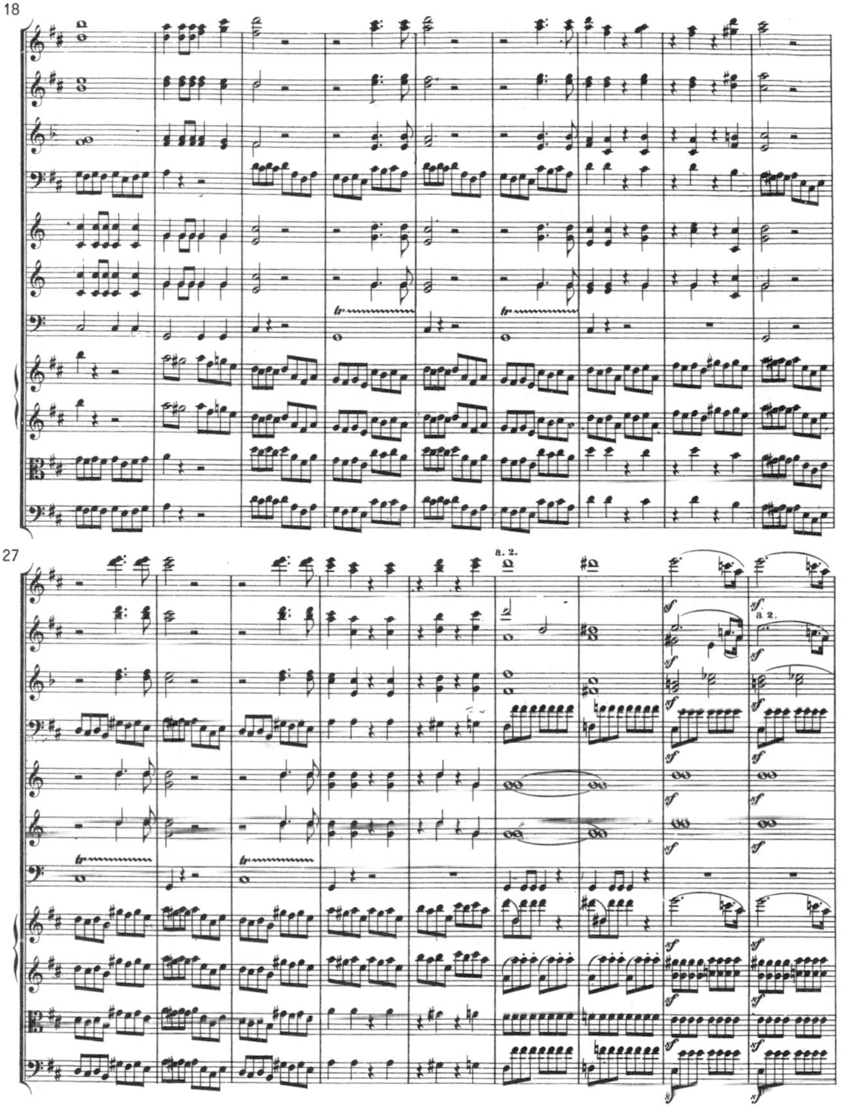
18
27
a. 2.
a 2.
tr
sf

77

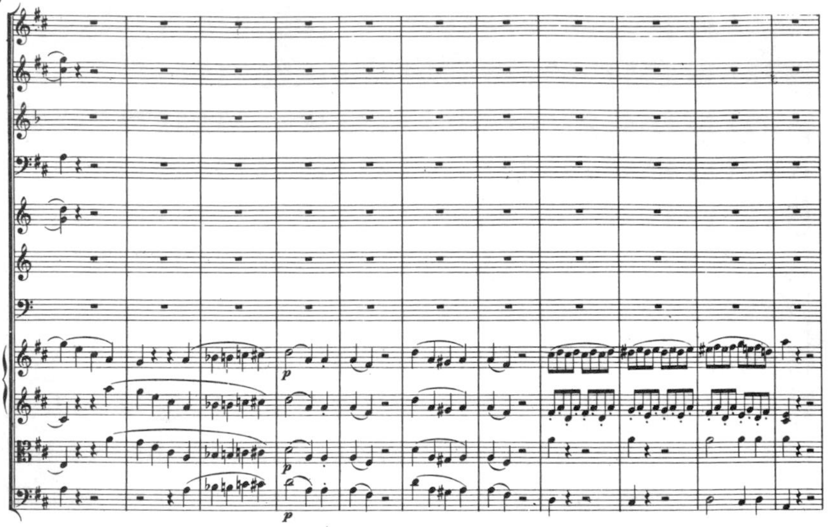

88

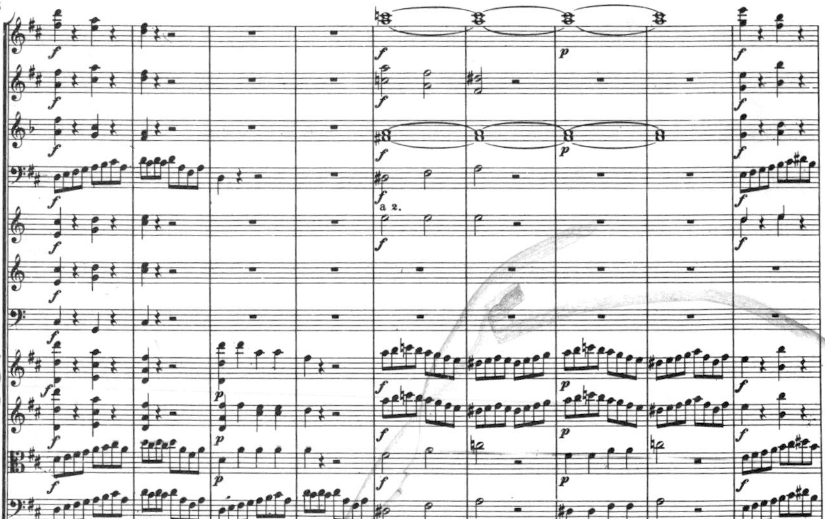

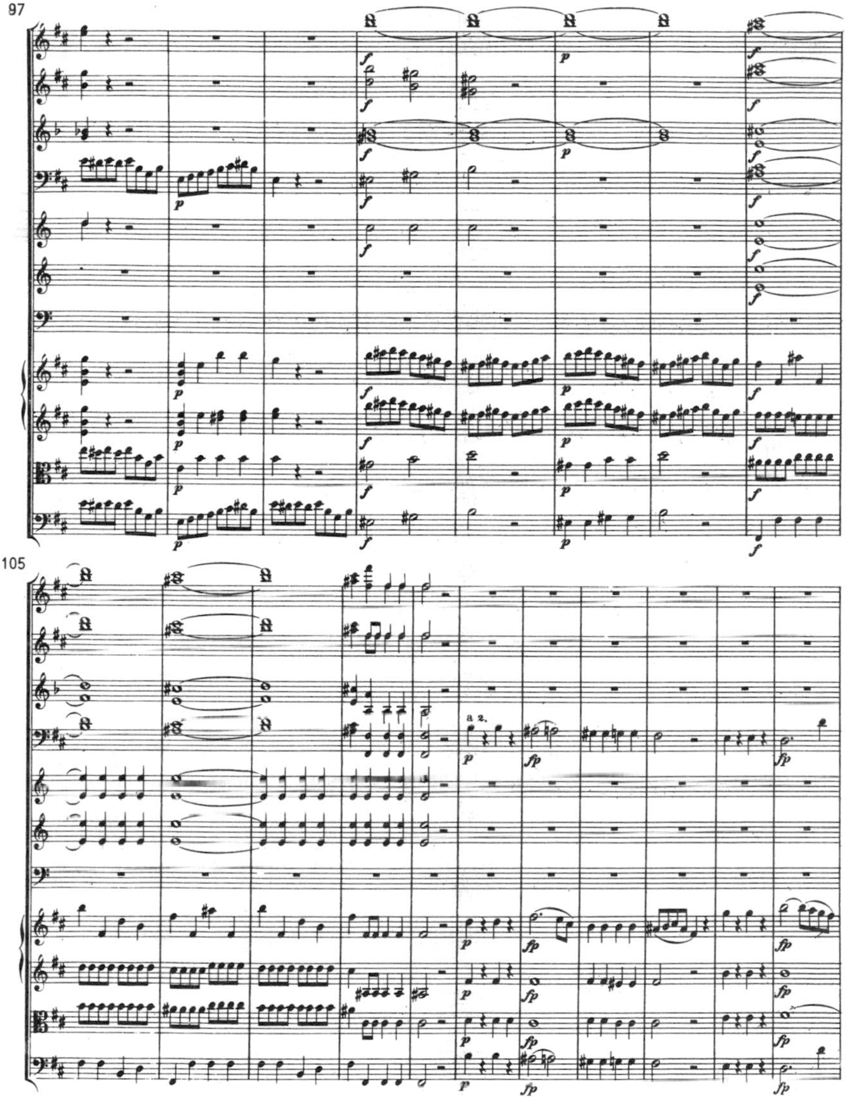
97
105
a 2.

116

124

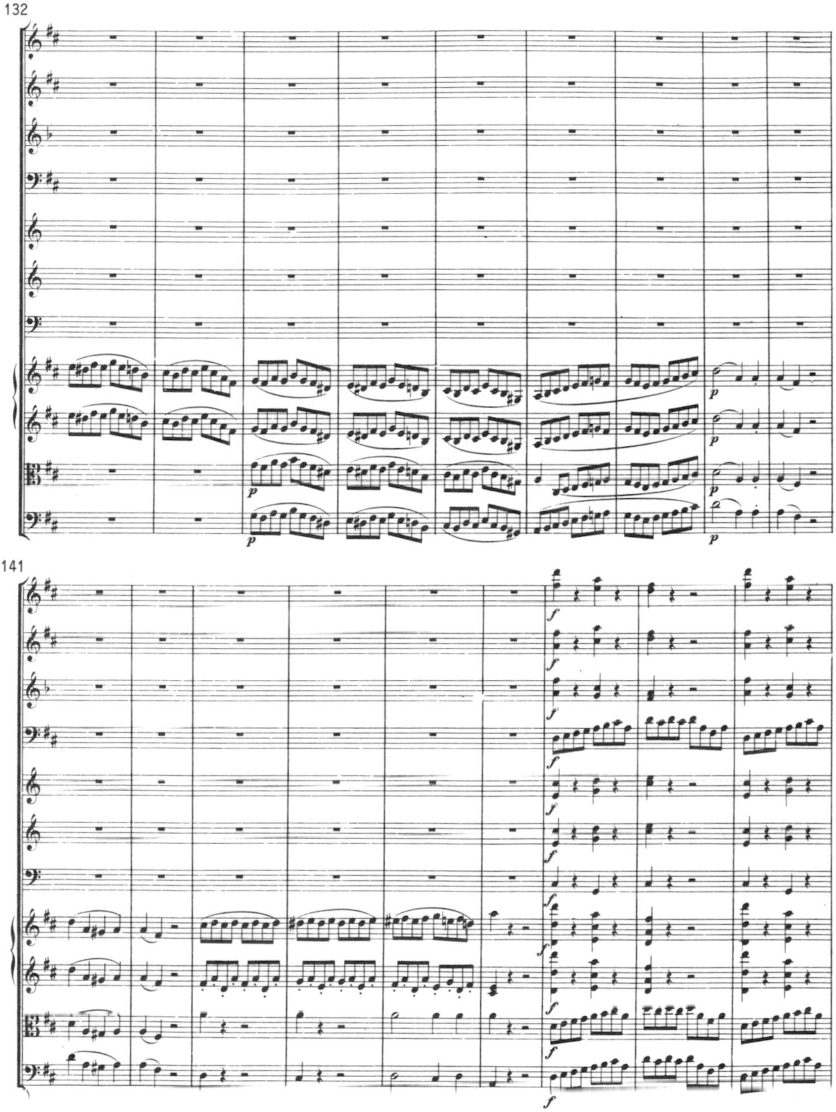
132
p
p
p
p
p
p
141
f
f
f
f
f
f
f
f
f
f
f

150

157

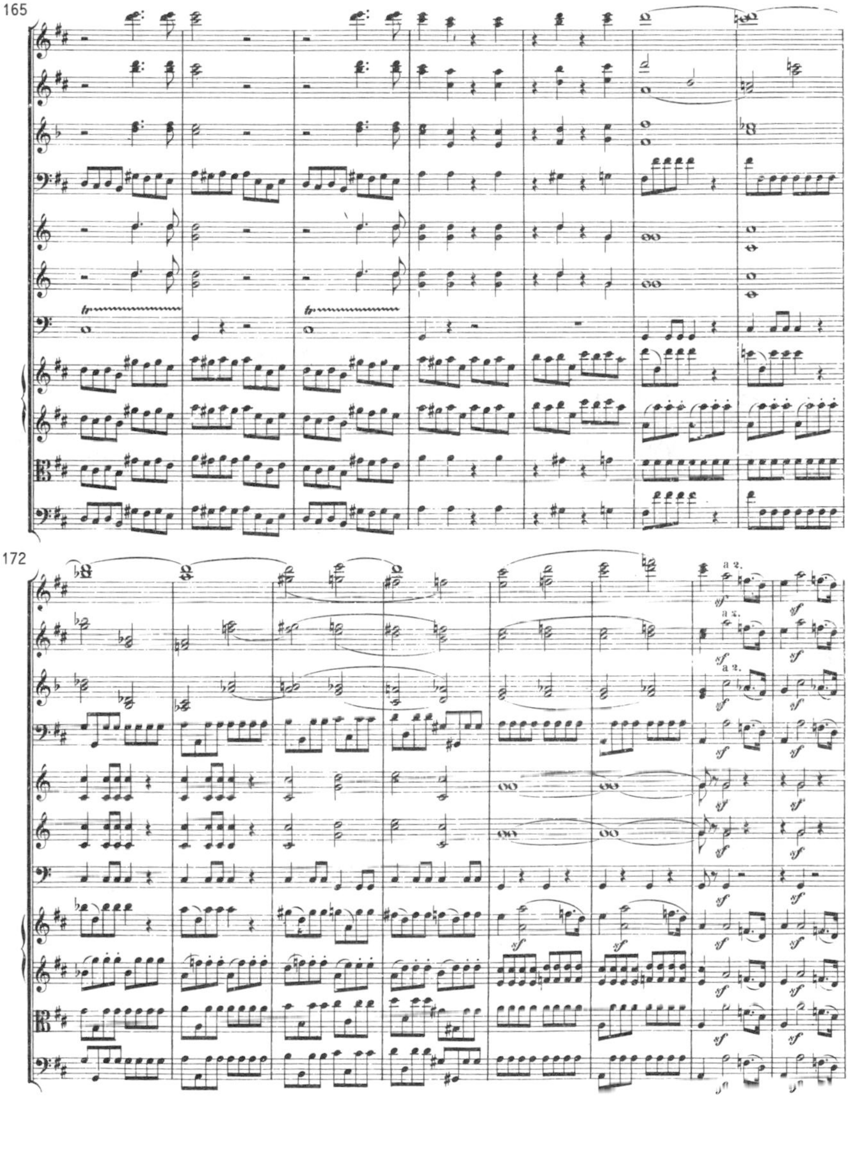
165
172
a 2.
sf

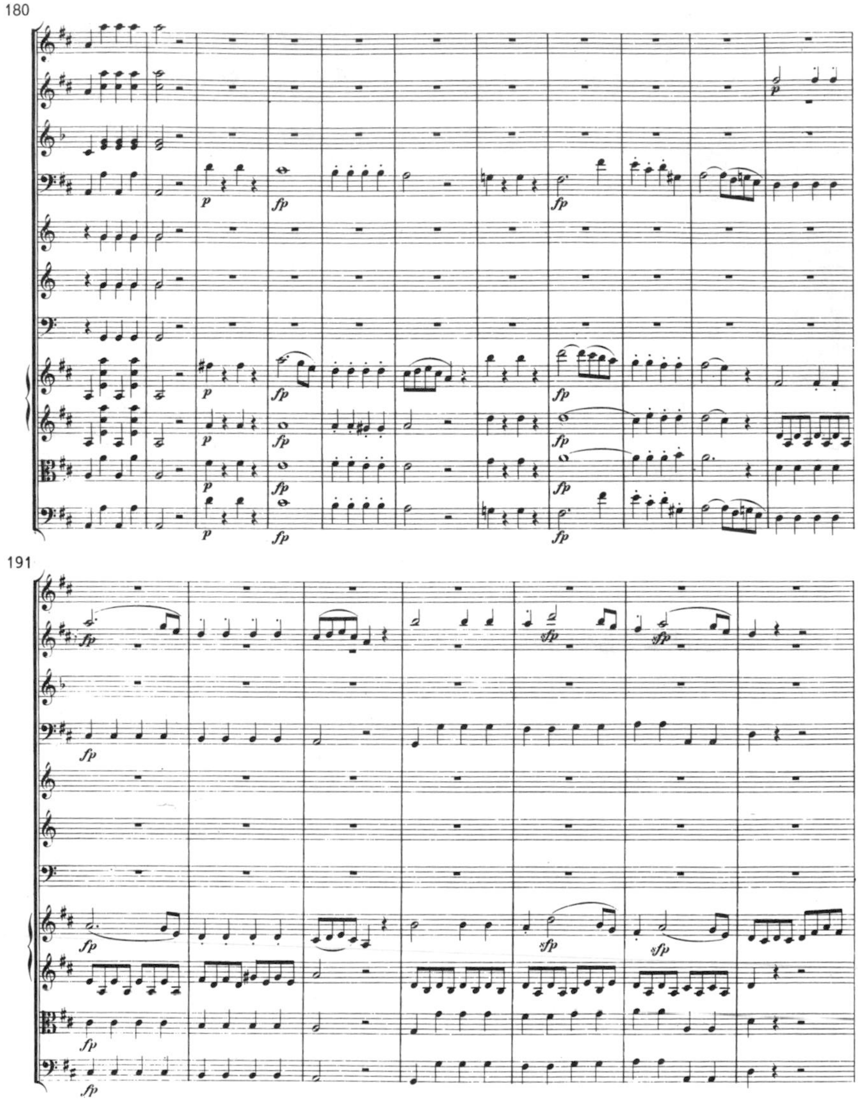
180
191

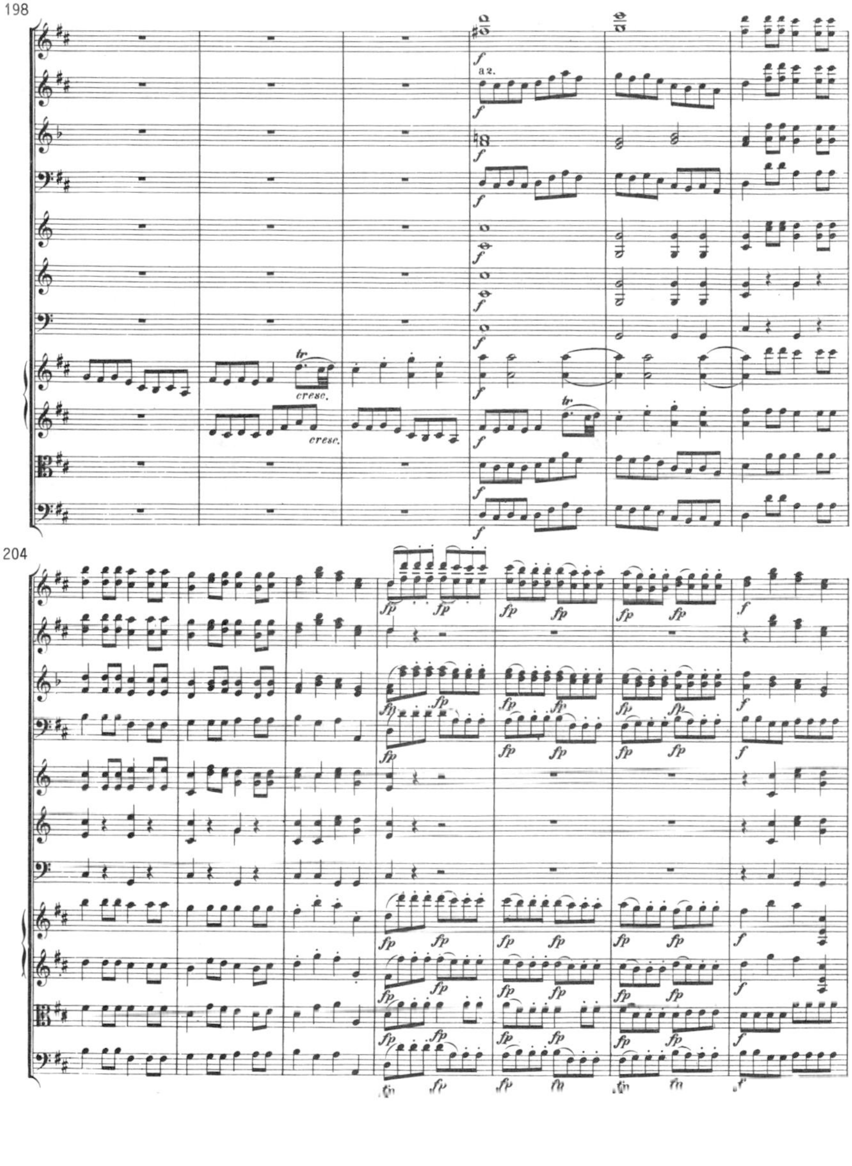
198
a 2.
cresc.
cresc.
204

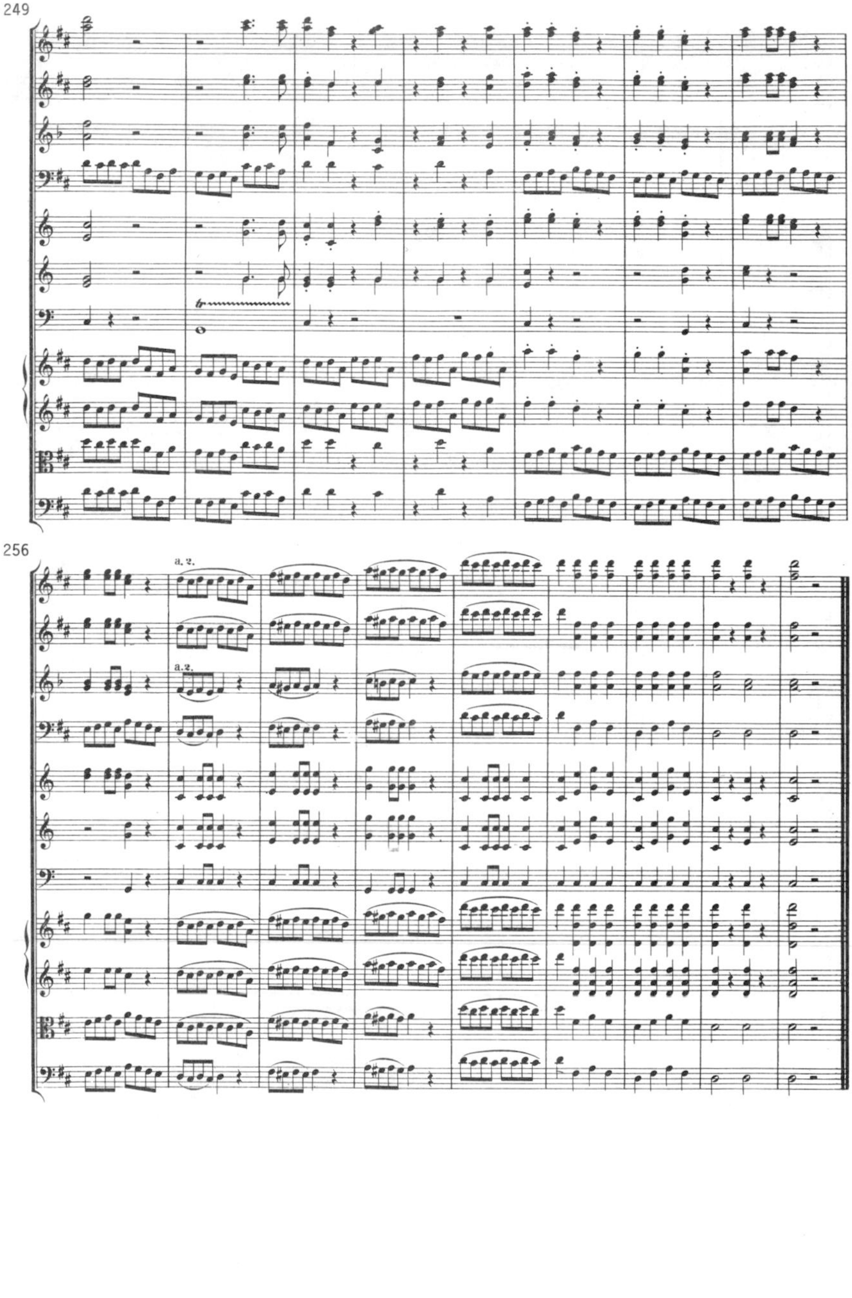
249
tr
256
a. 2.
a. 2.

Symphony No. 36

in C Major, K425, "Linz" (1783)

I

Allegro spiritoso.

154

165

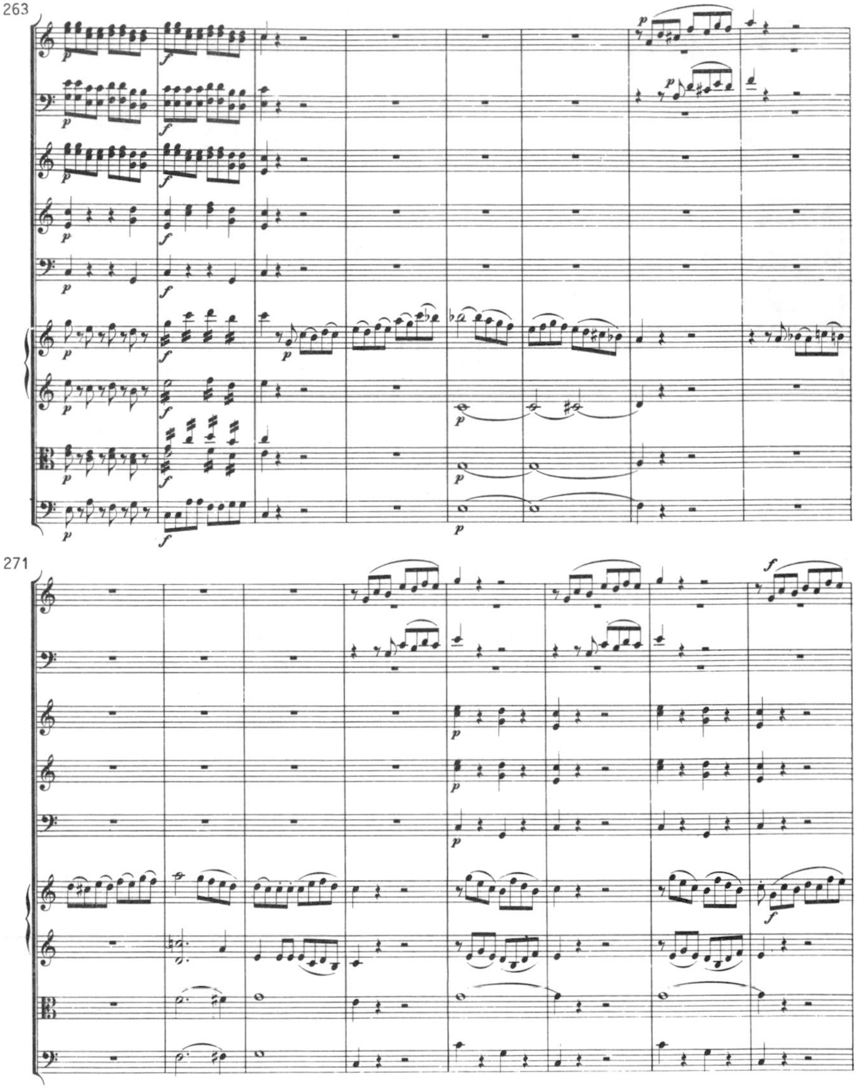
263
271

II

Poco Adagio.

Oboi.

Fagotti.

Corni in F.

Trombe in C.

Timpani in C.G.

Violino I.

Violino II.

Viola.

Violoncello e
Basso.

MENUETTO.

III

Oboi.	
Fagotti.	
Corni in C.	
Trombe in C.	
Timpani in C. G.	
Violino I.	
Violino II.	
Viola.	
Violoncello e Basso.	

227
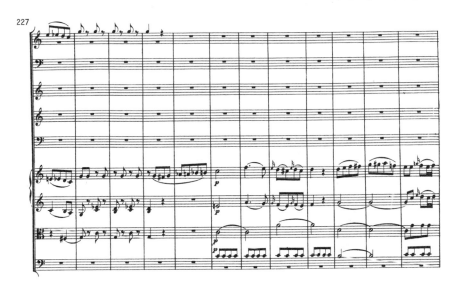

239

Symphony No. 38

in D Major, K504, "Prague" (1786)

I

47

55

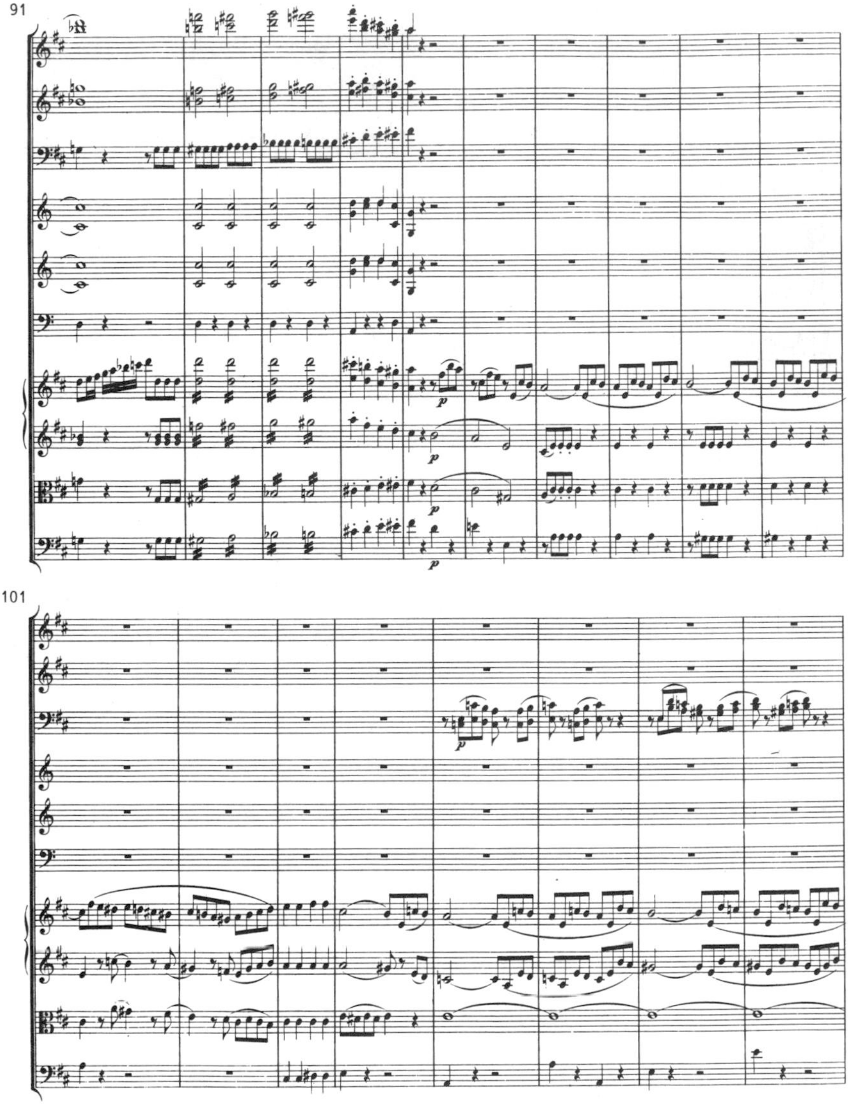
91
p
p
p
101
p

244

253

277

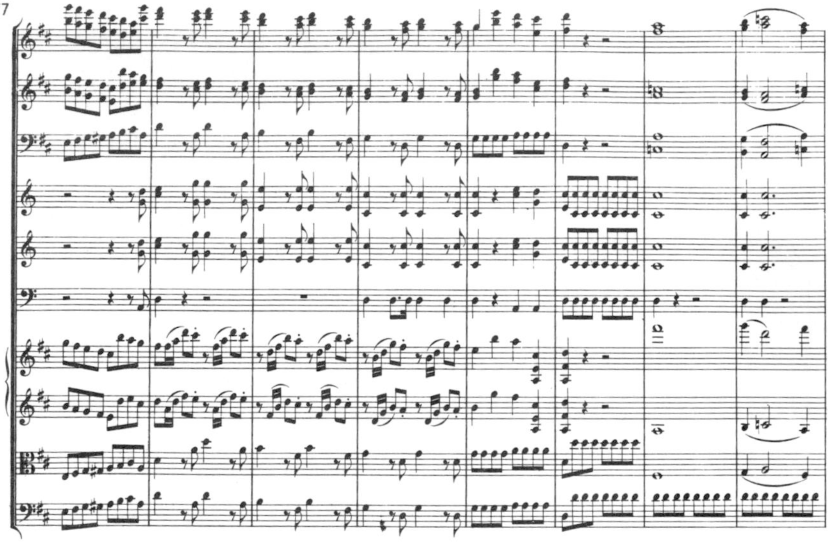

285

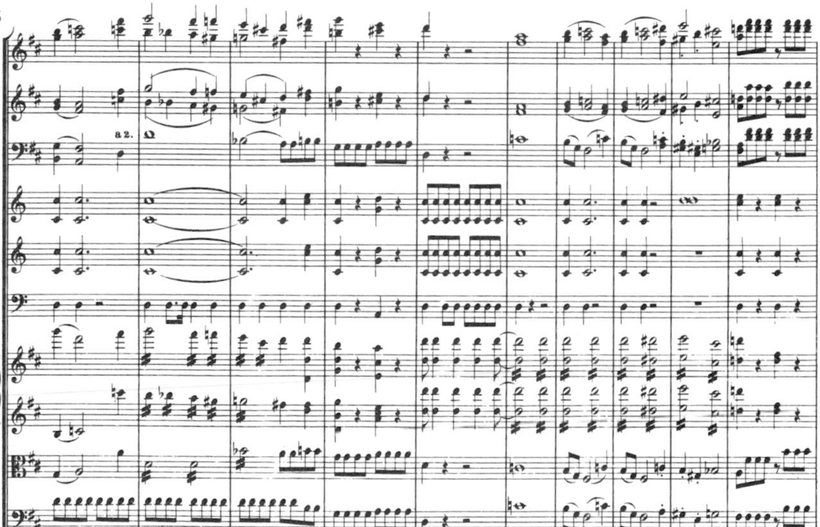

II

FINALE.
Presto.

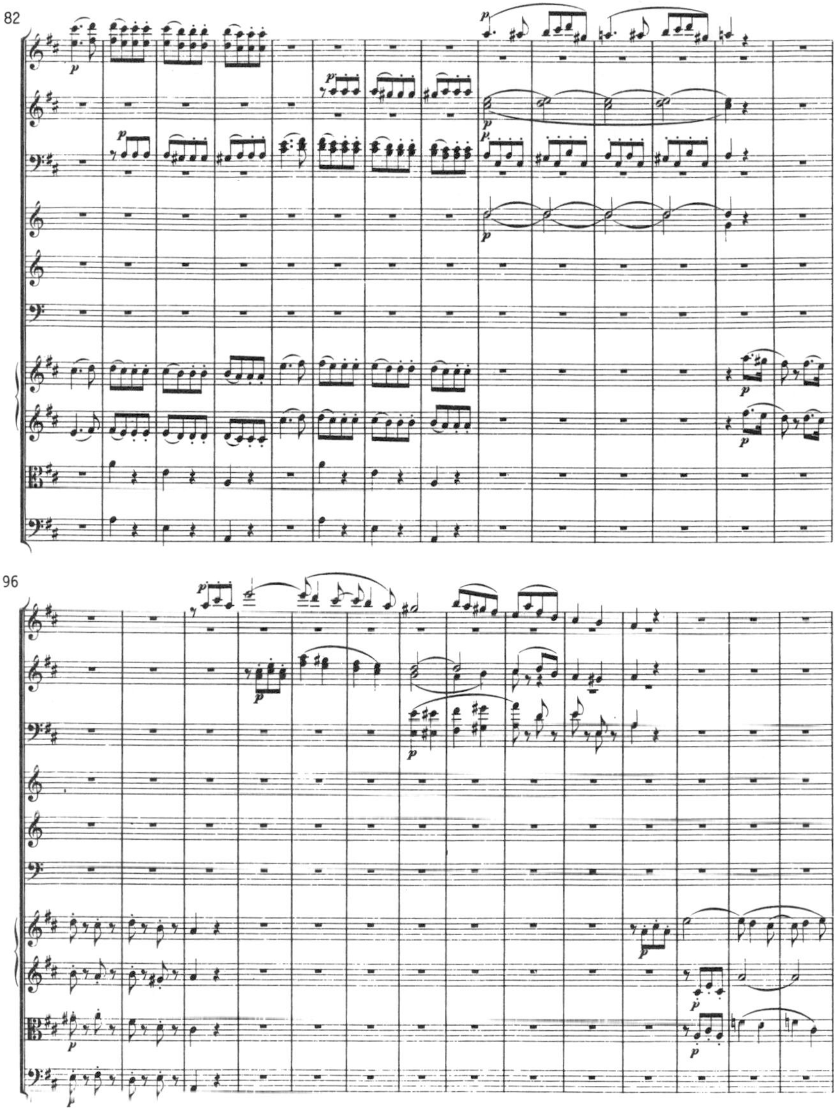
82
96

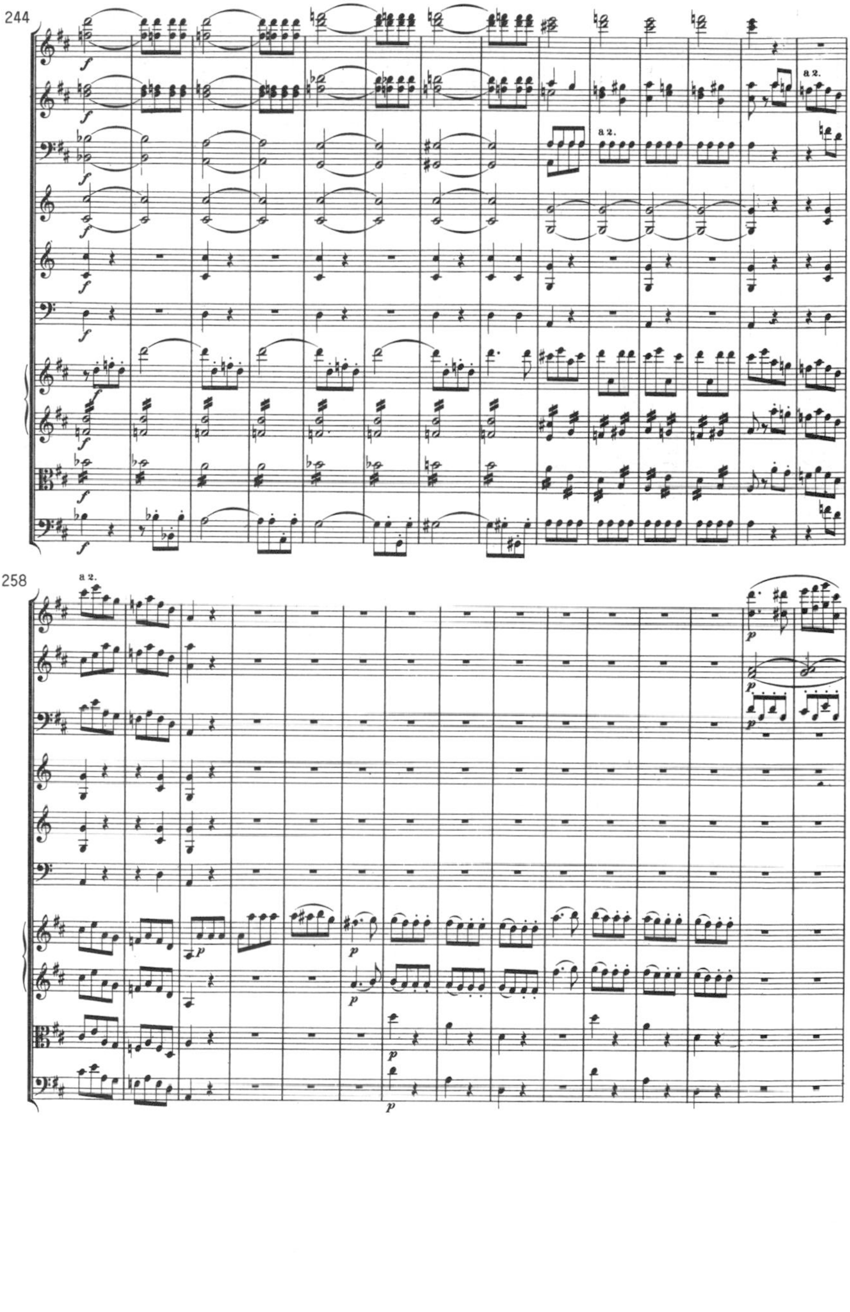
244
a 2.
a 2.
258
a 2.

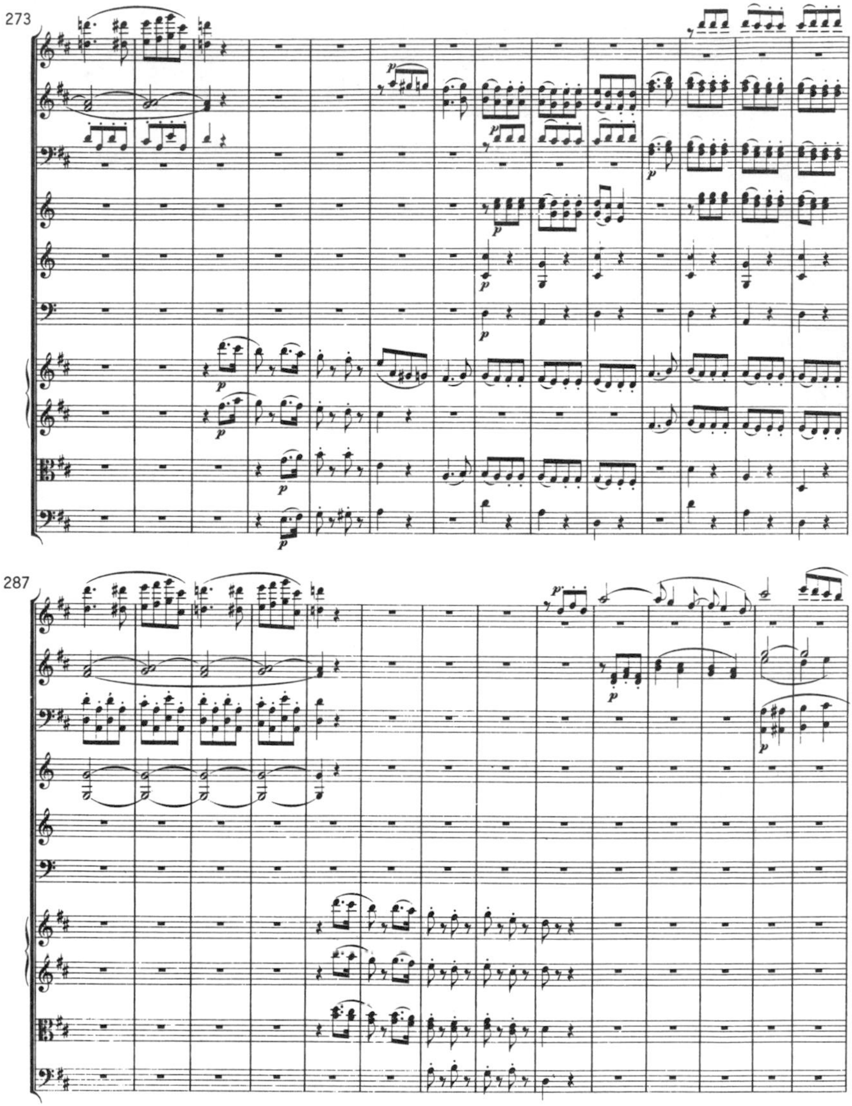
273
p
p
p
p
p
p
p
p
287
p
p
p

END OF EDITION

216 421
1076